FRANK LLOYD WRIGHT

THE EARLY WORK

Bramhall House · New York

0-517-N03743
Copyright © MCMLXVIII by The Frank
Lloyd Wright Foundation
Library Of Congress Catalog Card Number:
68-54184
This edition is published by Bramhall House,
a division of Clarkson N. Potter, Inc., by ar-
rangement with Horizon Press
a b c d e f g h
Manufactured in the United States of America

PUBLISHER'S NOTE

Wherever dates for the buildings were not given in the original German edition of *Ausgeführte Bauten* they have here been supplied; and errors in dates and captions have been corrected. The dates here given for the buildings are those that most closely refer to the time of their conception, as recorded on preliminary presentation drawings in the Taliesin archives carrying Frank Lloyd Wright's signature and date in his red square.

In the original German edition some of the illustrations appeared horizontally, others vertically. For this first edition in English the page size has been enlarged to permit all illustrations to be printed horizontally for convenient reference; and wherever original prints were still available and provided greater clarity, the reproductions in this edition were made directly from them.

The publishers wish to acknowledge the help of The Frank Lloyd Wright Foundation, Bruce Brooks Pfeiffer, Don Lovness, and Edgar Tafel in making original material available; and the help of W. R. Hasbrouck, the Chicago Architectural Photographic Company, and the Museum of Modern Art in supplying photographs.

"Frank Lloyd Wright, A Study and an Appreciation" is given in C. R. Ashbee's original English text, which, in the German edition, appeared only in German translation.

CONTENTS

INDEX TO THE ILLUSTRATIONS

INTRODUCTION

BY EDGAR KAUFMANN, JR.

Here is a reissue of *Ausgeführte Bauten*, originally published in Berlin by the firm of Ernst Wasmuth in 1911. The year before, Wasmuth's had published a great portfolio of Frank Lloyd Wright's buildings and projects; it held a sheaf of lavishly reproduced drawings, very personal in style, accompanied by the architect's comments.

The book here reissued was then presented; much smaller and paperbound, it showed photographs of what Wright had actually accomplished in twenty years of thoroughly principled, unconventional practice. A foreword was provided by C. R. Ashbee. Ashbee, who had known Wright for a decade, was a leader of the English arts-and-crafts movement and, thus, in the cultural avant-garde of his day. This small volume was planned to spread wider and to penetrate deeper in the world of European architecture than the costly and more mannered portfolio.

Why should alert intellectuals in Europe want to push the works and concepts of Frank Lloyd Wright, an American who until then had attracted only limited attention?

Dissatisfied with their academic systems, scanning the horizon for sources of creative vitality, Europeans were well aware of American efforts in the arts. Not only in literature: before the middle of the nineteenth century James Fenimore Cooper and Horatio Greenough had heralded the perfection of American tools and machinery; after seeing the evidence at international exhibitions European critics joined in the praise. Then, by the 1880's, Henry Hobson Richardson began to charm architects on both sides of the Atlantic into admiration and imitation of his brusque, free, but very sophisticated style, presented in powerful buildings with ample, carefully subordinated ornament. In 1893 the Chicago World's Fair drew hosts of curious Europeans to the New World. Most of those who cared for architecture were not much impressed by the orderly, snow-white central Fair buildings; this was cold-storage classicism. But around town they discovered the astonishing dynamism of skyscrapers, here (unlike those in New York) sometimes coherent, eloquent, even polished in their architectural expressions. The masterpiece of this art, designed by Louis Henry Sullivan, was in St. Louis; but in Chicago, by the same architect, stood the bulky, Richardsonesque Auditorium block, the slender, more original, and brand-new Schiller tower, and the dazzlingly decorated Transportation Building at the Fair. In all his works Sullivan used emphatic ornament, explicatory of the spirit of the structure it adorned, intricate and allusive. To Europeans, accustomed to seeing ornament as the key to architectural style, Sullivan appeared more advanced artistically than Richardson. Sullivan was given medals, and casts of his ornament went to museums from Paris to St. Petersburg. It is not surprising, then, that Europeans should continue to look for new talent in American architecture, particularly around Chicago.

Wright fulfilled these hopes. His design was more powerful than Sullivan's (under whom he had worked) and more supple than Richardson's. One could see that here was a rising succession of masters in American architecture, a new tradition. Moreover, Wright was clearly allied to the anti-academic arts-and-crafts movement, which, before its full flowering even in Europe, had taken root in the United States after the Philadelphia Centennial exhibition of 1876. By the 1890's the arts-and-crafts and the architecture sympathetic with them were so effectively developed in England that the Germans, envious of such symbols of cultural and social progress, determined to challenge the British in this as in every way. Their official investigator, Hermann Muthesius, published careful studies of English architecture over Wasmuth's imprint in 1902, 1904, and 1905. A parallel study of American architecture (by another hand) was so inadequate that only a portion appeared, in 1910. By then, a German invited to lecture at Harvard, Kuno Francke, seems to have convinced Wasmuth's that the most vital new American architecture was centered around Chicago and, in fact, led by Frank Lloyd Wright. To retrieve their error the publishers had but to seize this opportunity. Against the complex background of European interests Wright easily and willingly came to play a stellar role.

Late in 1909 Wright went to Europe; one of his main objectives was to arrange details of publication with Wasmuth's. Sometime the following year he visited his old friend, Ashbee, in England and asked him to write the foreword to *Ausgeführte Bauten* (so Ashbee informed Nikolaus Pevsner in 1939). Ashbee was a natural intermediary between Wright and the German-speaking world. An established light of the English artistic reform movement, he had recently designed important work for the leading German patron of progressive arts, the Grand Duke of Hesse. Ashbee, moreover, was exceptionally responsive to the aspirations and accomplishments of others, so much so that he could rarely bring himself to take sides (his essay here shows this almost ludicrously). Ashbee's links to America were older than those to Germany; the early silverware of his Guild of Handicraft is said to reflect the taste of a protean American, Charles G. Leland, inspirer of the Home Arts and Industries Association and its handbooks. From October 1900 through February 1901 Ashbee had travelled in the United States on a survey for the Council of the National Trust for Places of Historic Interest or Natural Beauty, who hoped to establish affiliations with like-minded Americans. In Chicago, Frank Lloyd Wright had actually agreed to act as secretary to an interested group, an improbable gesture that testifies to the power of Ashbee's charm. No doubt influence flowed in two directions, for after his Chicago trip Ashbee was surprisingly inclined to support sentiments that Wright announced in March of 1901 with his Hull-House lecture, "The Art and Craft of the Machine." Its ideas re-echo in Ashbee's essay for this book, naturally enough, only to be gently gainsaid at the end, with characteristic ambiguity.

Ashbee's vacillations did not affect younger European architects and designers. The influences of Wasmuth's Wright publications have been acknowledged and are visible in the earlier works of Walter Gropius and Ludwig Mies van der Rohe, to name only two chief examples. Later their former master, Peter Behrens, adapted Wright's designs, particularly ornamental details. From Holland an even older master, Hendrik Petrus Berlage, journeyed to the United States in 1911, the very year of *Ausgeführte Bauten*. He returned enthusiastic about Wright's buildings that he had visited, and this reaction colored the work of his students and their contemporaries in Holland. A succinct review of the situation has been given in Reyner Banham's *Theory and Design in the First Machine Age*. It is clear that his summation is correct in that Wright's greatest early works, the Larkin Building, Unity Temple, the Coonley, the Dana, and the Martin houses, were the first to affect European architects. It was in *Ausgeführte Bauten* that these men could approximate an actual experience of the buildings; those who could listen to Berlage (German was his second tongue) might further conceive the great role of space in Wright's architecture. Generally, however, Europeans came to focus on details of Wright's works. The more evidently influential details in *Ausgeführte Bauten* are worth some words of comment.

Wright's innovations, particularly those that could be seen as characteristic of machine processes in the service of architecture, aroused Europeans. Broad, simple features, without subtle modulations or adaptations, were understood by them in this sense. Where emphasis and fine scale were called for, they saw the features assembled and closely interrelated.

Wright's boldly rhythmic and intact wall masses, his sharp lines of mullioned windows laced with "electroglazed" ornament, and his square, dark trim strips, differentiating masses and planes, were among the details that attracted attention first; they show in many of the photographs presented.

Next, perhaps, came the challenge of roofs. As a rule, Wright's roofs were pitched more gently than those admired in northern Europe; still, the enfolding cover, which Ruskin had called architecture's glorified end, was handled with consummate skill in these works. Four designs presented here nevertheless terminated in flat, horizontal planes. The unprecedented Larkin office building, a compendium of machine-made modern architecture, was one. So, too, its artistic equal, the group of Unity Temple and Unity House, presenting new spatial and material daring. Further, there was a thrusting, shadowed, bluntly cubic house for Mrs. Gale; and a hieratic exhibition stand for a Universal Portland Cement display at Madison Square Garden. Thus, clear departures from traditional roof forms were embodied in two of Wright's most accomplished and mature designs, and in two of his most probing.

Now that the Larkin and Unity buildings have been mentioned, it must be said that they were more astonishing and challenging, especially abroad, than any of the residences. The Larkin in particular showed a whole new way of life, not only in the central, dentate pool of space and daylight shared by all inside, but in the entirely novel metal furniture, in the geometric trim, and the cheerful decorations. Moreover, the plain glass sheets at the entrances were as startlingly new as the energetic cascades of water outside were startlingly familiar: it seemed Wright could be inventive without losing a sense of the living past. Perusers of *Ausgeführte Bauten* could scarcely know of the Larkin Building's forced and filtered air, or its sound-absorbing surfaces; they could not fail to see how the fire stairs were made into architectural events by expressive separation and severe enclosures.

Unity was, in its requirements, more usual, but its expression was more extraordinary. Outside, it was as severe as the Larkin. Inside, Wright's use of trim to express his intentions reached new heights. In the Larkin interior, for instance, each post, crowned with ornament, has its entity not unlike a pillar in some classicizing order. Within Unity Temple's room, on the contrary, trim is devoted to celebrating relationships of space, deliberately at the expense of any massy entity. Much of this could not have come clear to Europeans until later. Nevertheless, some architectural abstract ornament of the 1910's and early 1920's has been related to Wright's, especially elaborate interiors by De Stijl designers. But these works achieve very different results; in them neither space nor mass is accentuated, rather, ornament can be said to exist as a third, independent element.

Unity Temple, with its heroic simplicity outside and its monumental integrity inside, was admired and studied in Europe. This attention was aroused in part by Wright's masterful handling of a recalcitrant material, concrete. Some of his technique was suggested by a full-page photograph showing form-work, and in others the quality of exterior surfaces could be sensed. No one could match this foray into the new architectural terrain; not the Perrets, whose garage building of 1905-06 was intrinsically lesser, nor de Baudot with his earlier, gawky, but more directly comparable St. Jean de Montmartre.

Space, the dominant theme of Unity, was explored variously in a dozen buildings in the book. Like the buildings already mentioned, interlocking of major and minor spaces into richly variegated vistas occurs in the great Dana House and its gallery (both still standing and furnished as shown), and in the lesser Evans, Roberts, and Baker houses. The last two show particularly neat and well finished examples of the "studio" living room with balcony, later popular with Continental architects for more restricted buildings.

Nine other houses, ranging from quite modest to quite elaborate ones, raised main floors above ground level in a way that must have reminded Europeans of the *piano nobile.* Wright's motives, to gain view and air on the flat prairie, were different from the motives of cleanliness and commerce underlying the European system, yet in both cases a certain dignity resulted. Especially noticeable are the dramatic entrance stair and the main rooms it leads to in the Tomek House, all designed with a surer architectural touch than the same elements in the more famous Robie House, illustrated in the book (though Banham thought not). The Robie House benefits from better materials and a finer exterior, especially in the expression of its subordinate parts; but in spatial essentials the Tomek House is clearly superior.

In these two houses chimney masses and stairs gently screen living from dining areas. In several others living and dining areas are more directly conjoined, in a way that again had later Continental echoes; see the smaller Martin House, and the Horner and Hickox houses. Unification of spaces for the sake of spaciousness was further emphasized by Wright's favorite expository device, his trim. Often the dotted lines on plan (i.e., ceiling patterns) show relationships less legible in the photographs. Unification achieved or explained by trim would not fail to recall the rococo to Europeans, however remote Wright's forms from any such. Similarly, the frequent use in plan of extended and opposed axes, nodular octagons, and lesser details appears related to neo-Gothic usages. There is little doubt that Wright inherited these devices from that era by way of American examples.

Wright's interiors, especially those not in homes, seem to have provided European designers with a motif that became a preoccupation. A clear separation of parts, relating them without interfering with the integrity of each, is called "Elementarism" by Banham, who sees in it a distinct phase of modern European structural expression. For Wright the playful suppression of meaningful joints was admissible only for minor decorative accessories or for display purposes. If Wright's example encouraged this trend in European work it must have been through the photographs of his exhibition installations and his bookshop and art-gallery interiors; e.g., the light fixtures in Browne's. This side of Wright's work reveals more than any other, I think, his acknowledged debt to the formal qualities of Japanese prints and — more obviously — to the lamps and grilles they sometimes portray and which he had encountered in real life when he visited Japan in 1905. Europeans were no less alert than he to these oriental stimuli; a common ground was shared.

Thus, *Ausgeführte Bauten* could achieve its intended aims in many ways, some of them minor but lasting. Neither it nor the more extensive portfolio, nor travelers' reports from Berlage and Ashbee, could do more than whet the Europeans' appetite for more, and more direct, experience of the American creativity they saw in Wright. That, in fact, was the next story, but it does not belong here.

Ausgeführte Bauten was first published more than a half century ago. It was not well known in the United States at that time, nor was its companion, the portfolio; a series of accidents kept them from distribution here, as Wright has told in *An Autobiography*. The aims and impact of *Ausgeführte Bauten* in Europe were traced in the preceding paragraphs. What are the uses of this reissue, at this time and in the United States? It will be welcomed of course by those who love Wright's work and by those who like to document tides of cultural influence. But a more profound result could be hoped for, too; this book may now in some ways affect American architects and their art. In the right hands it may be grafted onto current practice as a sprig of rich, cultivated olive is spliced into a wild stock rooted in the soil. One element supplies survival, the other adds quality. This book might be such a cion.

FRANK LLOYD WRIGHT.

UNITY TEMPLE UNDER CONSTRUCTION, OAK PARK, ILL. 1905

MODEL OF UNITY TEMPLE

FRANK LLOYD WRIGHT
A STUDY AND AN APPRECIATION BY C. R. ASHBEE

In the modern development of the arts America excels in the art of Architecture, and there are few cities upon the great continent but can show some piece of good building, or an effort in that direction; it is a popular instinct. The rich man strives to mark his wealth in stone, the cities have great libraries, clubs, colleges and schools, the states vie with one another in the splendour of thir state-houses. Into spheres in which with us the architect seldom penetrates, he in America leaves his mark; the office and business building has become his province.

The names of many of the leading architects in the last two generations have been well enough known in Europe: Richardson, Hunt, McKim, Mead and White; Cope and Stewardson; Day, Clipston Sturges, Carrere and Hastings, Cass Gilbert, and many others. The buildings of these men will take their place in the sequence of architectural history; the libraries at Boston, and Washington, the Statehouses of Pittsburg and Providence, the Metropolitan Club in New York, the collegiate buildings in Philadelphia, in Cambridge, in San Francisco.

To us, who look at them with the eyes of the old world, American buildings connote four things in style. They stand first for the English tradition, whether through the "old Colonial" or more recent importation of English forms; the French "Beaux Arts" as we see it in Washington or Fifth Avenue, New York; the purely utilitarian as in that distinctly American Business Product, the "sky scraper;" and they stand lastly for what may be called the buildings of a new spirit, as we see it on the Pacific coast and in the Middle West. It is of these last as expressed by the work of Frank Lloyd Wright that I wish specially to speak, because he first and before all other American architects seems to embody it.

3

This new spirit has for us in Europe a peculiar charm and piquancy, just because we do not see in it that reflection of European forms to which we have been so long accustomed. Its characteristics are a departure from tradition, a distinctiveness of surrounding, and a consequent character of its own, a delight in new materials, and an honest use of machinery. There are features that give to the buildings of the Pacific coast a character quite distinct from the School of Chicago as the conditions are not the same, and I have been in houses on the Arroyo that appeal to me more than Frank Lloyd Wright's; but all the men of the new spirit have these characteristics, and the work of Frank Lloyd Wright has them fundamentally and more markedly than any of his contemporaries. This is not to be wondered at, because it has grown within it own province — the sphere of the Middle West — and is something absolutely new and original. Trained in the office of Louis Sullivan, who first gave rational character to the industrial building of Chicago, Frank Lloyd Wright has carried the new spirit into domestic work and produced a type of building that is absolutely his own. In so doing he has given to the great city of the Prairie something she had never had before, and what is equivalent to a new architecture.

In estimating the achievement for which Wright stands, we have to consider the difficulties he had to face. With no background of tradition, with no forms about him upon which to model a style, surrounded by purely commercial conditions, and in the face of actual and fierce hostility, or the persecutions of "that little knowledge which is a dangerous thing," he carved out a manner of his own and worked out his own principles of design, before the English Arts and Crafts Movement, the German Secession, or the European Art Nouveau had in any way touched America. His Winslow House (p.19) was designed in 1893, and other of his buildings in which the elements of his style are in formation bear approximately early dates. I sum up the characteristics of his work thus: first, nobility of plan — some of Frank Lloyd Wright's plans have the cleanness and simplicity we see in the planning of Gothic houses, or in the work of Bramante; then a fine proportion, witness the Oak Park houses (p. 28, etc.) with their long firm horizontal lines. Next, a feeling for mass and colour, as in the Unity Temple (p. 14) and the Coonley house (p. 118); a fertility of resource in adapting means to ends; and lastly a determination, amounting sometimes to heroism, to master the machine and use it at all costs, in an endeavour to find the forms and treatment it may render without abuse of tradition. In a suggestive and interesting monograph which he contributed in 1908 to the "Architectural Record" of New York, entitled 'In the cause of Architecture,' Frank Lloyd Wright laid down the principles that inspired his work. From among them I am tempted to extract the following because it is so significant of the work and what it stands for:

"Buildings, like people, must first be sincere, must be true and then withal as gracious and lovable as may be."

"Above all, integrity. The machine is the normal tool of our civilization; give it work that it can do well — nothing is of greater importance. To do this will be to formulate the new industrial ideals we need if Architecture is to be a living Art."

Here we are brought face to face with the problem of our civilization, the solution of which will determine the future of the Arts themselves. It is significant that from Chicago, quite independently of England, of France, of Germany or elsewhere, here is a voice calling, offering a solution.

"An artist's limitations are his best friends. The machine is here to stay. It is the fore-runner of the Democracy that is our dearest hope. There is no more important work before the architect now than to use this normal tool of civilization to the best advantage, instead of prostituting it as he has hitherto done in reproducing with murderous ubiquity forms born of other times and other conditions, and which it can only serve to destroy."

There is greatness in this idea, and the future will I think show that, in the case of Frank Lloyd Wright, the man's product has been worthy the idea that has guided its development and in a measure inspired its creation. Out of it has come a different conception as to what constitutes a modern building.

Greatness demands its price, and this has often to be paid in a certain barrenness and sterility of detail owing to the severity of the limitations, a certain disregard of the intimate and personal things that make a building lovable in the sacrifice of tenderness for integrity. This is not so much the fault of the architect as of the conditions in which he is set to work. The machine is not yet mastered in modern life, nor is it possible for any individual, however strong, to accomplish the mastery. This is the community's need, a social need, and it is one which we feel essentially in the Art of America.

Through the United States indeed the traditions of craftsmanship, upon which the arts professedly rest, have been broken down by mechanical power more than with us in Europe, and the American Architects, with all their greater organizing power, their combinations, and their opportunities which are supreme, have not yet devised a way of re-establishing them, of finding their equivalent, of readjusting the balance. It is to the credit of Frank Lloyd Wright that he is the first American architect who has sought to consciously express this fact, to readjust this balance. He is thus a typical product of modern America, and of that aspect of America which is Chicago. He

TERRACOTTA FIGURE AT ENTRANCE TO SUSAN L. DANA HOUSE. FRANK LLOYD WRIGHT, ARCHITECT RICHARD BOCK, SCULPTOR

has its strength as well as its weakness, its romance as well as its freakishness and immaturity, its barrenness as well as its sanity, its fertility of resource, and he has perhaps in an exaggerated degree its individualism. I use the word as Murray defines it, of self-centered conduct or feeling as a principle, and mode of life, in which the individual pursues his own ends or follows his own ideas. I do not know why this individualism takes its extremest form in Chicago. Every street, every avenue of that great-souled and generous, but at the same time brutal and remorseless, city tells of this. It tells somehow of the New Englander driven westward and unrestrained, in a commercial world; of the Puritan cut adrift from his gods and from his conventions, striving to make new ones out of himself. "Striving," as Blake the Seer put it, "with systems to deliver individuals from those systems." I see this striving in the work of Frank Lloyd Wright more than in any of his contemporaries.

The result is what has been called the style of the Middle West, and after accounting for him in his relation to Louis Sullivan, that style is more of his making than that of any other man. Destiny permits a man to strive, mocks him in his struggle, and in the end collects some of the fragments — that which was best and most enduring — for the greater work that is to remain. Thus styles are made, and this is so of architecture before all the arts. One may pardon in a strong man a display of individualism that one cannot forgive in a weaker; what is the character in the one becomes pettishness, or mannerism or affectation in the other; but we artists of Europe, while we appreciate and criticise the product, and while we often admire, may be forgiven when we say that in our feeling it sometimes needs to mellow. Yet whatever we may think of this individualism, and however it may win or repel us personally, it expresses for the time being a national condition. For my own part, speaking as an architect, I think this individualism, as seen in Frank Lloyd Wright's work, strong and sound

SUSAN L. DANA HOUSE, SPRINGFIELD, ILL. ENTRANCE

to the core; there is in it a national ideal, but I do not always like it. It gives me at times the same feeling of irritation which Walt Whitman gives me, when, after some supreme passage at which one's whole heart goes out, the poet tumbles over some trifle badly handled, as when, for instance, in that subliment of his songs, "Come, I will make the continent indissoluble," he ends up with the words "For you, Oh Democracy, MA FEMME!" He forgets that we are of the same flesh and blood, and have a sense of humour; that this trivial note tumbles us from the sublime, into detail that is badly done. I do not mean to insinuate by this example that Frank Lloyd Wright's work has inconsistence of this nature; the analogy cannot of course be pressed, and the deduction applies only to my own personal feeling regarding the sometimes undigested trivialities I find. I hold moreover that his work is architecture, while it merits the comparison, in greatness and unity, with Whitman's work in literature, is quite strong enough to stand a corresponding criticism of its limitations or its faults.

A comparison of the work of Frank Lloyd Wright with modern work in England or Germany would take me too far afield; but a certain kinship is significant and may be referred to in passing. In Germany the names of Olbrich, Hoffman, Moser, Bruno Paul, Mohring suggest themselves. In England those of us who are sometimes called the Arts and Crafts men, Lethaby, Voysey, Lutyens, Ricardo, Wilson, Holden, Blow, Townsend, Baillie Scott. We feel that between us and him there is a kinship. We may differ vitally in manner of expression, in our planning, in our touch, in the way we clothe our work, in our feeling for proportion, but although our problems differ essentially, we are altogether at one in our principles. We guard in common the lamp of truth. We hold equally with Frank Lloyd Wright that structure should be self-explanatory, that iron is there for man's service, only he must learn to use it rightly, and not learn to lie or cheat about it, that the forms of the ancient world, the traditions of the "Beaux Arts," and the old Colonial, even 'Greek purism' have their place, but that their place is not necessarily the Prairie. Their place may be Connecticut, or Virginia, may be the Boulevard Montparnasse, or Buckinghamshire, but for the great open spaces of the new world something else is wanted. This land, pierced by the great trunk lines of the Middle West, the new cities of the miners, the cattlebreeders, the canners and the grain exporters, the men of ideas and invention, make a new appeal. The men who have created it, however we may view them, stand for something new, and the time is ripe for a new form to express the life they lead, or toward which they may aspire. And this life is a large life, it has given to the work of Frank Lloyd Wright that unity of idea, that largeness which his plans and drawings reveal. I have seen it, too, in such buildings as the Coonley House near Chicago (p. 118) and the Larkin Building in Buffalo (p. 128 ff.). It is the architect's business to express life, and to ennoble it in the expression. Frank Lloyd Wright has done this; and yet all the honour is not his. To see these buildings, or think through these drawings, brings home to one how much he owes his clients. They have felt the greatness themselves, and have themselves sought to become articulate. No one can study the simple and convincing forms of the Larkin Building in Buffalo (pp. 128-141) without a feeling that bigness in business organization has called forth a corresponding mood in the architect.

We artists ourselves are too apt to think that we are the discoverers of forms that come new to us. It is not so. We ourselves are but the instruments through which breathes the Over-soul, the Zeitgeist. Those rapid nervous lines, those big masses, this sense of a new proportion, this breaking away from old traditions, this monotony that results from constant

mechanical repetition, this longing for individual expression as a refuge from it; we all have this in our work, and it has its psychological reason. Industrial concentration, rapid locomotion, the telephone, the electric light and the lines it demands, mechanical power which has enormously cheapened and as equally permeated certain conditions of labour, the breakdown of the old productive system, the photograph, the telegraph, the development of the press and more particularly the illustrated press, these and many others are the influences that unconsciously move us all, and make us speak, puppets that we are, in ways we do not know, and, what seems so strange to each of us individually, make us speak with a common voice. Thus again, styles are made, and the style of the 20th century can never have real quality if it does not somehow express those influences behind the life of the time.

So far Frank Lloyd Wright has been given but little opportunity in public building, but in what he has done he has left his mark. No one can look at the Unity Temple in Oak Park, its monumental character, its frank revival of the temple form as best suited to a place of modern worship, its method of construction, solid monolith, cast in concrete, reinforced with steel strands, a construction that will last for hundreds of years after the whole suburb has passed away, without a sense that here is the new spirit, and distinctively American.

On the Romanesque churches of the old world, later generations set the mosaic, the tracery, the refinement and the culture that came with more leisure and sympathy; another century may do the same with the great experiments in architecture that America is putting forth. I have seen buildings of Frank Lloyd Wright's that I would like to touch with the enchanted wand; not to alter their structure in plan or form, or carcass, but to clothe them with a more living and tender detail. I do not know how, and the time is not yet—nor would I like to see Wright do it himself, because I do not believe he could; for thus to clothe them would mean a school of Craftsmanship that would tell of the intimate life of America, and imply a little of that quietude and poetry and scholarship which our English churches and country houses have received from the caressing hands of generations of craftsmen. Here at all events, witness these pages, the buildings are, and they are worthy of the life. Morris said to me once, in praise of noble decoration, "we do not want it at all unless at the outset buildings upon which we place it are noble." In the buildings of Frank Lloyd Wright that postulate is granted.

AVERY COONLEY HOUSE, RIVERSIDE, ILL.

Mit hungrigen Blicken ſchauen wir europäiſche Architekten häufig auf die glücklicheren Kollegen in der Neuen Welt mit ihren herrlichen Geländeverhältniſſen und ihren weiten Strecken unbewohnten Landes, ihren Städten, die noch des Künſtlers harren, und auf die Freigebigkeit der Bauherren für den erforderlichen Aufwand. Aber all das neiden wir ihnen weniger als den Hauch neuen Lebens, das, nicht gefeſſelt von Tradition und Sitten, ſo viel friſcher pulſiert als bei uns, wo wir die Feſſeln fühlen, ſobald wir in Holz und Stein, in Eiſen und Beton unſeren Gedanken Ausdruck geben wollen. Der Grund dafür iſt leicht zu erſehen, denn wie verſchieden geſtaltet ſich doch das Leben eines amerikaniſchen Bauherrn von dem eines europäiſchen Magnaten, wieviel freier, ungebundener, getragen von größeren Ideen, aber auch, das muß geſagt werden, wieviel gewöhnlicher, ja vielleicht ſogar roher. Euer Amerikaner wünſcht große Zimmer, ausgedehnte Räume von gleicher Temperatur; er wünſcht Konzentration, die Haſt iſt ihm Lebenselement, ihm fehlt der Sinn für Muße, dagegen hat er Verſtändnis für die koſtſpieligen Arbeiten des Rohrlegers, und mit wahrhaft kindlichem Eifer kauft er in Europa an bric a brac, was er irgend an ſich bringen kann.

Ganz anders die, die in England und Deutſchland über große Vermögen gebieten, ihnen ſind engere Grenzen gezogen. Der begüterte deutſche Bourgeois fühlt über ſich des Kaiſers nicht nur ſchirmende Hand. Er liebt ſeinen Kaiſer möglicherweiſe gar nicht, aber der Kaiſer hat eine Uniform und iſt der Repräſentant einer anderen Dimenſion, er iſt wie eine größere leuchtende Erſcheinung außerhalb der realen Dinge, etwas Unerreichbares, ſchimmernd in Farben und Gold.

In England iſt es das Houſe of Lords mit ſeinen Fallſtricken; hier herrſcht das Milieu des Landjunkers, und ſ c h w e r l a ſt e t ſein Einfluß auf dem Bau und der Ausſchmückung des Hauſes. Ein engliſcher Gentleman würde glauben, daß er ſehr niedrig ſtehenden koſtſpieligen Paſſionen huldige, wenn er die Rechnung eines amerikaniſchen Rohrlegers begleichen würde, die bei einem großen Gebäude allerdings viele tauſend Mark betragen kann. Er würde fürchten, daß die Diſziplin der Domeſtiken erſchüttert und ſeine Pferde in ihren heiligſten Gefühlen verletzt werden könnten.

Ebenſo verſchieden ſind die Verhältniſſe bei öffentlichen Gebäuden. England iſt von den drei genannten Ländern das demokratiſchſte, wobei ich das Wort im Sinne Abraham Lincolns verſtehe, Dentſchland zeigt die ſtraffſte Diſziplin, und in Amerika herrſcht unbeſtritten die Macht des Geldes oder des Mannes, der es beſitzt. Die Folge iſt, daß bei dem Bau unſerer öffentlichen Gebäude die Komitees, in denen die kleinen Ladeninhaber ſitzen, den Ausſchlag geben; in ihrer Gedankenſphäre herrſcht der Groſchen, und ſo kommen wir denn zu den Errungenſchaften, deren Anblick uns oft genug ſo melancholiſch ſtimmt. In Amerika herrſcht das „boss system", das ja oft, wenn auch nicht immer, den fähigſten Mann an die Spitze bringt, während andererſeits in Deutſchland eine feſtgefügte Tradition das öffentliche Leben beherrſcht, die ſich denn auch in ſeinen Gebäuden ausprägt.

Es erſcheint vom pſychologiſchen Standpunkt ganz folgerichtig, daß die eben ſkizzierten Kräfte dem Leben in den drei Ländern ihren Stempel aufdrücken, und wir müſſen die gemeinſamen Grundlagen durchforſchen, wenn wir nach verwandten Zügen ſuchen.

These passages were reproduced directly from the original edition and are retained in German because they were not included in C. R. Ashbee's original English text.

Es geschieht absichtlich, wenn ich mich über die Einzelheiten der Innenarchitektur Lloyd Wrightscher Bauten nicht verbreite, denn darin scheint mir der Schwerpunkt seines Schaffens nicht zu liegen, er ist dafür nicht typisch. Um es noch einmal zu wiederholen, man erkennt darin den Kampf um die Maschine, ihrer will er Herr werden, und darin liegen auch die Grenzen seiner Kraft.

Häufig gelingt es, japanischen Einflüssen auf die Spur zu kommen, wir sehen, wie er bestrebt ist, japanische Formen den amerikanischen Bedingungen anzupassen, wenn der Künstler selbst diesen Einfluß auch nicht zugestehen will. Zweifellos ist der Einfluß des Ostens ein unbewußter, aber ich sehe ihn in den meisten seiner architektonischen Zeichnungen und in der Art, wie er das malerische Element in seinen Bauten zur Geltung bringt. Diese seine Bauten haben für mich einen großen Reiz, und einige Abbildungen in diesem Hefte gewähren einen Begriff von seinen Leistungen auf dem Gebiet der inneren Ausstattung, und zwar in den verschiedensten Materialien, wie Glas und Stoffe; auch Teppiche und Möbel hat er geschaffen, und man kann all diesen Einzelheiten die Anerkennung nicht versagen, daß sie logisch sich dem Bauwerk anpassen, aber sie legen jedenfalls für unseren europäischen Geschmack nicht so überzeugend Zeugnis von seiner Persönlichkeit ab wie seine Bauwerke selbst. Seine Prinzipien sind aber auch hier vornehmer Natur; sie treten uns am klarsten aus den eigenen Worten des Künstlers entgegen. Er sagt:
„Um ein Bauwerk, seine Umgebung und seine innere Ausstattung zu einem harmonischen
„Ganzen zu gestalten, muß man darauf hinwirken, daß das Zubehör sich dem Gesamt-
„zweck unterordnet, mag es nun künstlerischen oder praktischen Zwecken dienen, das
„Bauwerk als Ganzes muß es absorbieren, und es ist Sache des Architekten, dafür zu
„sorgen, daß es sich der wahren Natur des Bauwerks anpaßt. Das ist das Hauptbe-
„tätigungsfeld für den modernen Architekten, er muß es verstehen, das Bauwerk zu einem
„in sich geschlossenen harmonischen Kunstwerk zu gestalten, das das Handeln und Fühlen
„seiner Bewohner getreulich widerspiegelt und so zu einer Künstleroffenbarung wird, bei
„der die Persönlichkeit aus dem Material und seiner Anordnung hervorleuchtet.“

BAS RELIEF, LARKIN BUILDING, FRANK LLOYD WRIGHT, ARCHITECT
RICHARD BOCK, SCULPTOR

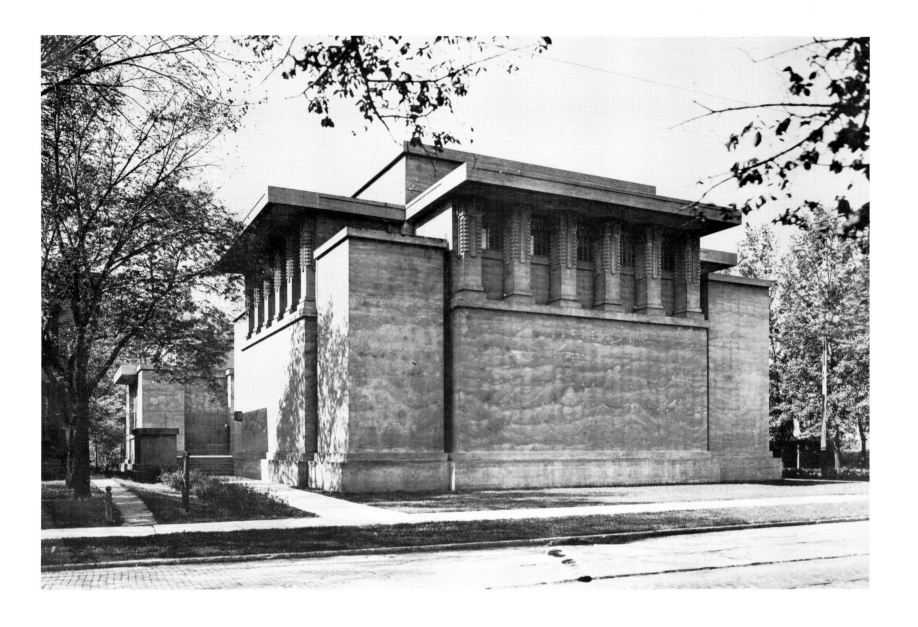

UNITY TEMPLE, OAK PARK, ILL.

UNITY TEMPLE AND UNITY HOUSE, OAK PARK, ILL.

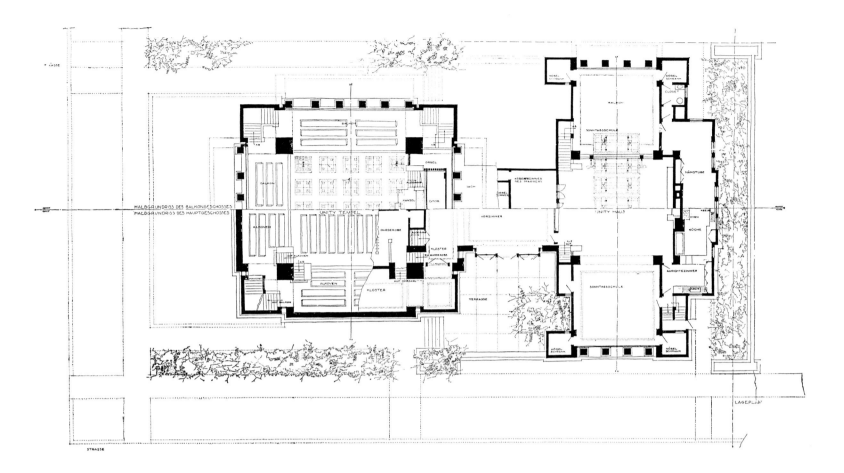

UNITY TEMPLE AND UNITY HOUSE, OAK PARK, ILL. PLAN

UNITY TEMPLE AND UNITY HOUSE, OAK PARK, ILL.

(ABOVE) UNITY TEMPLE, WEST SIDE
(BELOW) UNITY HOUSE, WEST SIDE

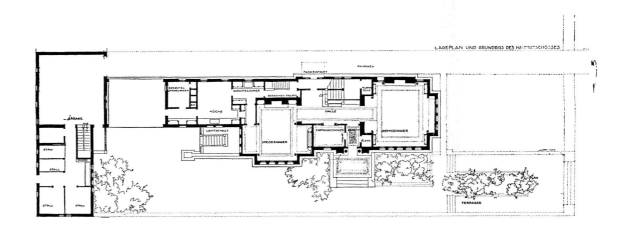

(ABOVE) UNITY TEMPLE, OAK PARK, ILL. INTERIOR
(BELOW) ISIDOR HELLER HOUSE, CHICAGO, ILL. 1896. PLAN

ISIDOR HELLER HOUSE, CHICAGO, ILL.

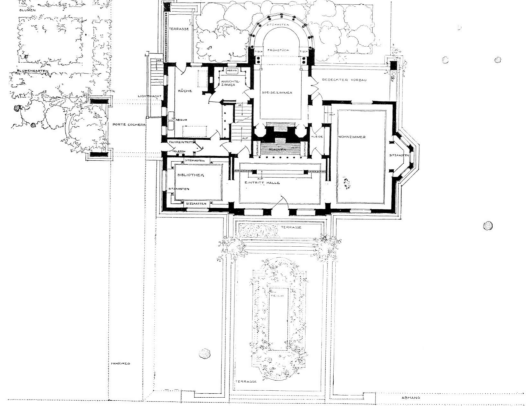

W. H. WINSLOW HOUSE, RIVER FOREST, ILL. 1893. ENTRANCE AND PLAN

W. H. WINSLOW HOUSE, RIVER FOREST, ILL.

JOSEPH HUSSER HOUSE, CHICAGO, ILL. 1899

JOSEPH HUSSER HOUSE, CHICAGO, ILL. WEST SIDE AND SOUTH SIDE

CHAUNCEY L. WILLIAMS HOUSE, RIVER FOREST, ILL. 1895

B. HARLEY BRADLEY HOUSE, KANKAKEE, ILL. 1900

B. HARLEY BRADLEY HOUSE, KANKAKEE, ILL. ENTRANCE WAY AND DINING ROOM

B. HARLEY BRADLEY HOUSE, KANKAKEE, ILL. LIVING ROOM

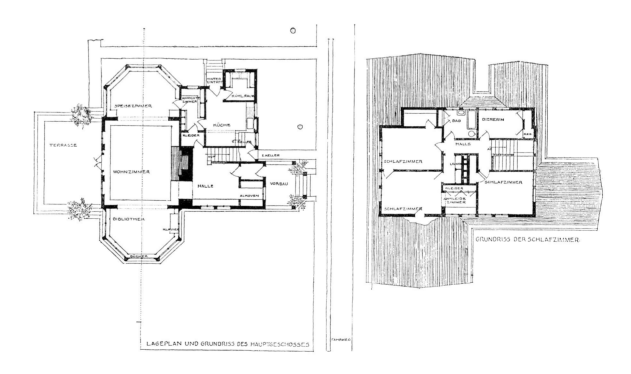

WARREN HICKOX HOUSE, KANKAKEE, ILL. 1900. SOUTH SIDE AND PLANS

WARREN HICKOX HOUSE, KANKAKEE, ILL. EAST SIDE

FRANK THOMAS HOUSE, OAK PARK, ILL. 1901

FRANK THOMAS HOUSE, OAK PARK, ILL. DETAILS, EAST SIDE

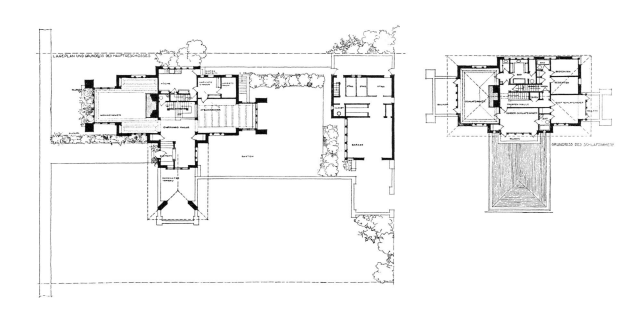

FRANCIS W. LITTLE HOUSE, PEORIA, ILL. 1902. STREET VIEW AND PLANS

FRANCIS W. LITTLE HOUSE, PEORIA, ILL.

SUSAN L. DANA HOUSE, SPRINGFIELD, ILL. 1903

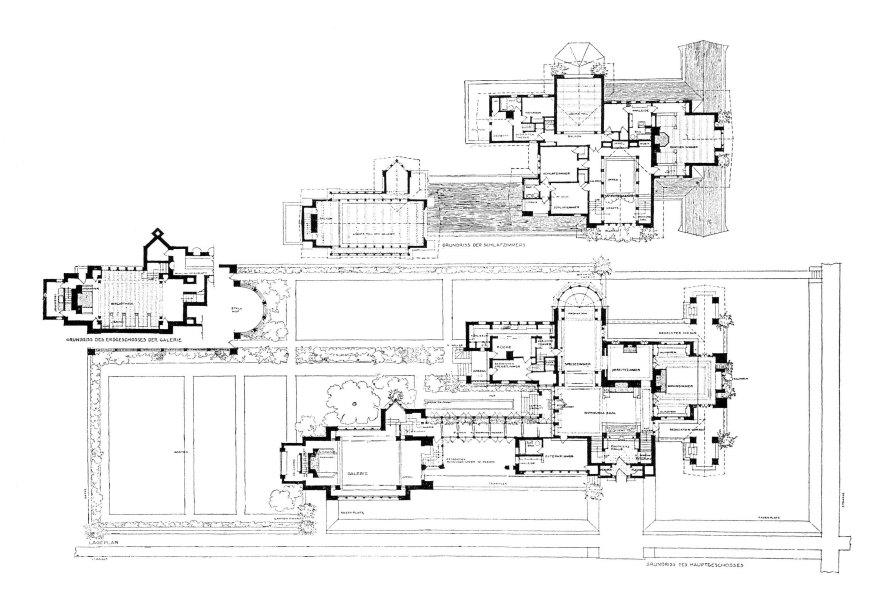

SUSAN L. DANA HOUSE, SPRINGFIELD, ILL. PLANS: MAIN FLOOR AND UPPER FLOOR

SUSAN L. DANA HOUSE, SPRINGFIELD, ILL. SOUTH SIDE

SUSAN L. DANA HOUSE, SPRINGFIELD, ILL. DETAILS, ENTRANCE

SUSAN L. DANA HOUSE, SPRINGFIELD, ILL. DINING ROOM

SUSAN L. DANA HOUSE, SPRINGFIELD, ILL. FOUNTAIN IN DINING ROOM

SUSAN L. DANA HOUSE, SPRINGFIELD, ILL. DINING ROOM AND BREAKFAST NOOK

SUSAN L. DANA HOUSE, SPRINGFIELD, ILL. EAST SIDE

SUSAN L. DANA HOUSE, SPRINGFIELD, ILL. EAST SIDE

SUSAN L. DANA HOUSE, SPRINGFIELD, ILL.
GALLERY AND DIVIDING DOOR

SUSAN L. DANA HOUSE, SPRINGFIELD, ILL. GALLERY EXTERIOR

SUSAN L. DANA HOUSE, SPRINGFIELD, ILL. INTERIOR OF GALLERY

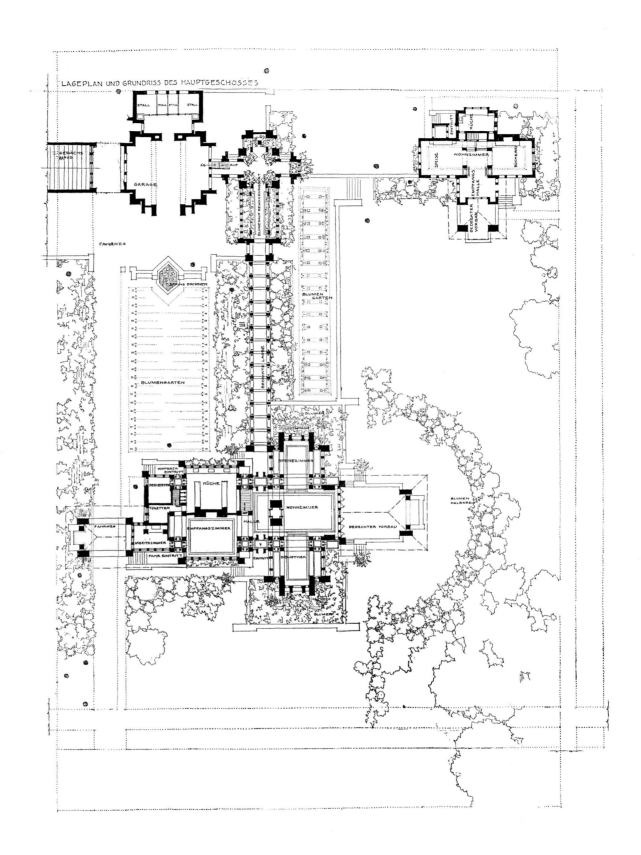

DARWIN D. MARTIN HOUSE, BUFFALO, N.Y. 1904. PLAN OF MAIN FLOOR

DARWIN D. MARTIN HOUSE, BUFFALO, N.Y. BIRD'S EYE VIEW

DARWIN D. MARTIN HOUSE, BUFFALO, N.Y.

DARWIN D. MARTIN HOUSE, BUFFALO, N.Y.
GREENHOUSE AND RADIATORS (CONCEALED BEHIND BOOKCASES)
WITH LIGHTING FIXTURES

DARWIN D. MARTIN HOUSE, BUFFALO, N.Y.
PERGOLA AND ENTRANCE HALL

DARWIN D. MARTIN HOUSE, BUFFALO, N.Y.
GREENHOUSE AND BIRD HOUSE ON ROOF

DARWIN D. MARTIN HOUSE, BUFFALO, N.Y.
(ABOVE) RECEPTION ROOM AND (BELOW) DINING ROOM

51

DARWIN D. MARTIN HOUSE, BUFFALO, N.Y.
WEST SIDE AND DETAIL OF WEST SIDE

DARWIN D. MARTIN HOUSE, BUFFALO, N.Y.
LIVING ROOM WITH RADIATORS (CONCEALED BEHIND BOOKCASES) AND LIGHTING FIXTURES

DARWIN D. MARTIN HOUSE, BUFFALO, N.Y.

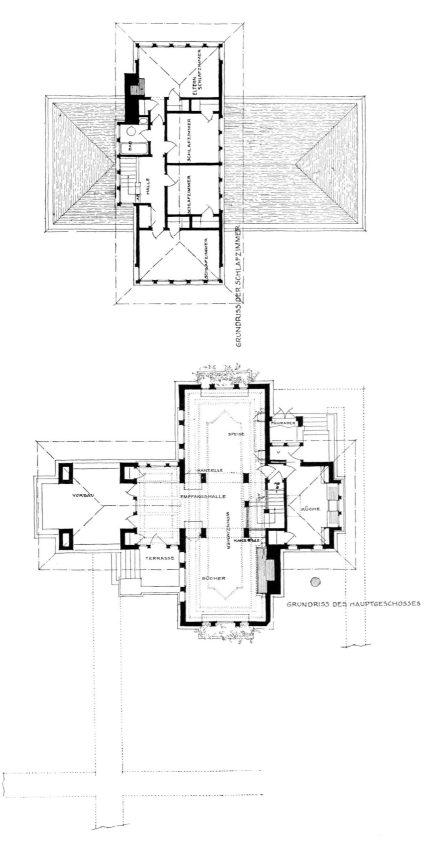

DARWIN D. MARTIN HOUSE, BUFFALO, N.Y.
PLANS: (ABOVE) UPPER FLOOR AND (BELOW) MAIN FLOOR

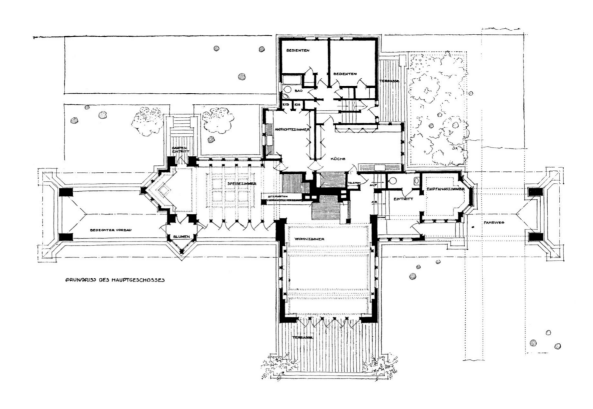

GRUNDRISS DES HAUPTGESCHOSSES

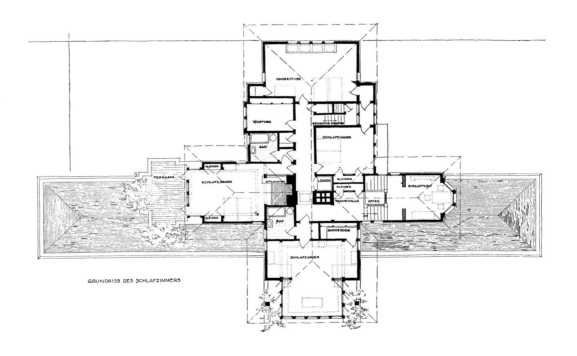

GRUNDRISS DES SCHLAFZIMMERS

WARD W. WILLITS HOUSE, HIGHLAND PARK, ILL. 1901
PLANS: (ABOVE) MAIN FLOOR AND (BELOW) UPPER FLOOR

WARD W. WILLITS HOUSE, HIGHLAND PARK, ILL.

WARD W. WILLITS HOUSE, HIGHLAND PARK, ILL. STREET SIDE

WARD W. WILLITS HOUSE, HIGHLAND PARK, ILL. ENTRANCE WING AND LIVING ROOM

OSCAR STEFFENS HOUSE, CHICAGO, ILL. 1909

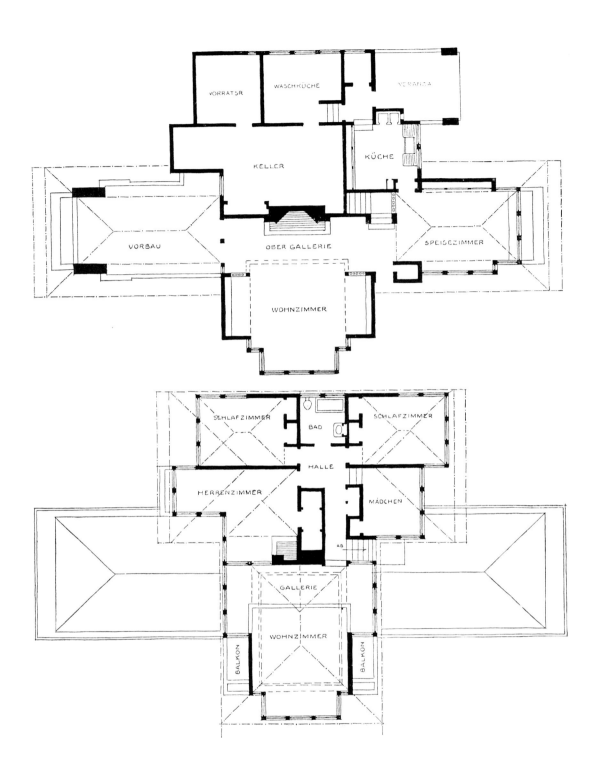

OSCAR STEFFENS HOUSE, CHICAGO, ILL.
PLANS: (ABOVE) UPPER FLOOR AND (BELOW) MAIN FLOOR

L. K. HORNER HOUSE, CHICAGO, ILL. 1908
EXTERIOR AND INTERIOR OPPOSITE ENTRANCE

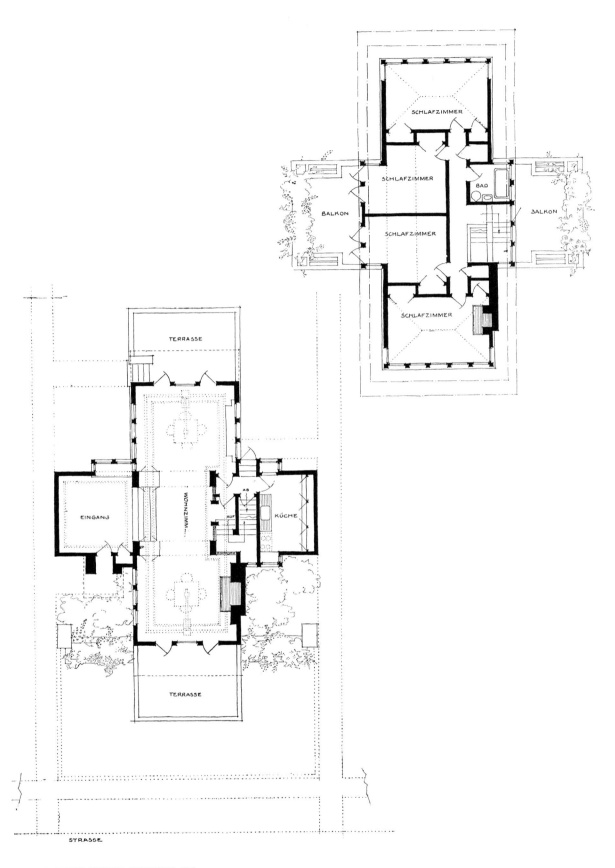

L. K. HORNER HOUSE, CHICAGO, ILL.
PLANS: (ABOVE) UPPER FLOOR AND (BELOW) MAIN FLOOR

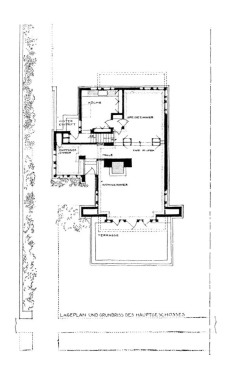

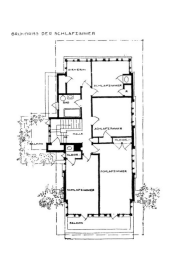

MRS. THOMAS H. GALE HOUSE, OAK PARK, ILL. 1909. STREET VIEW AND PLANS

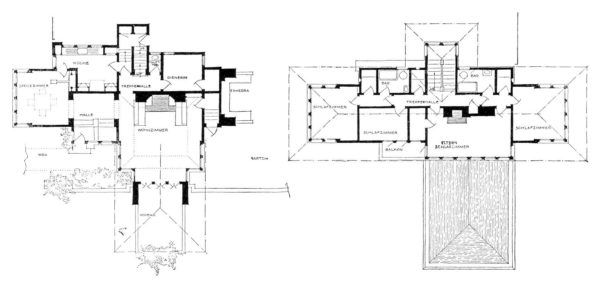

GEORGE MILLARD HOUSE, HIGHLAND PARK, ILL. 1906. VIEW AND PLANS

ISABEL ROBERTS HOUSE, RIVER FOREST, ILL. 1908

ISABEL ROBERTS HOUSE, RIVER FOREST, ILL. SOUTH SIDE AND LIVING ROOM

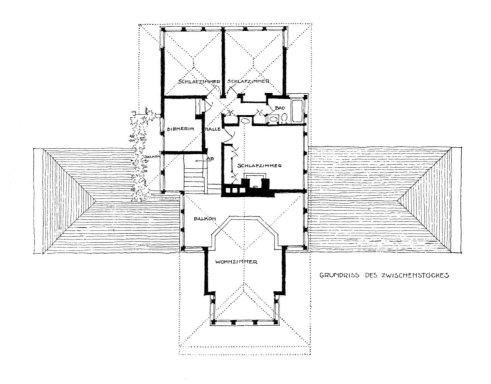

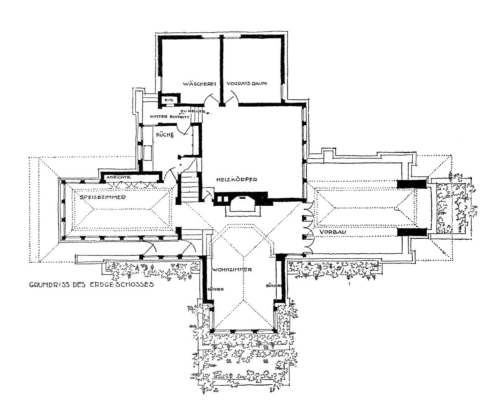

ISABEL ROBERTS HOUSE, RIVER FOREST, ILL.
PLANS: (ABOVE) UPPER FLOOR AND (BELOW) MAIN FLOOR

68

W.E. MARTIN HOUSE, OAK PARK, ILL. 1903
TWO VIEWS OF GARDEN SIDE

F. F. TOMEK HOUSE, RIVERSIDE, ILL. 1907. STREET (SOUTH) SIDE

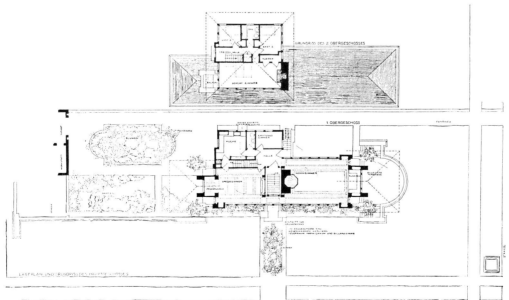

F. F. TOMEK HOUSE, RIVERSIDE, ILL. PORCH AND PLANS

EMMA MARTIN HOUSE, OAK PARK, ILL. 1907

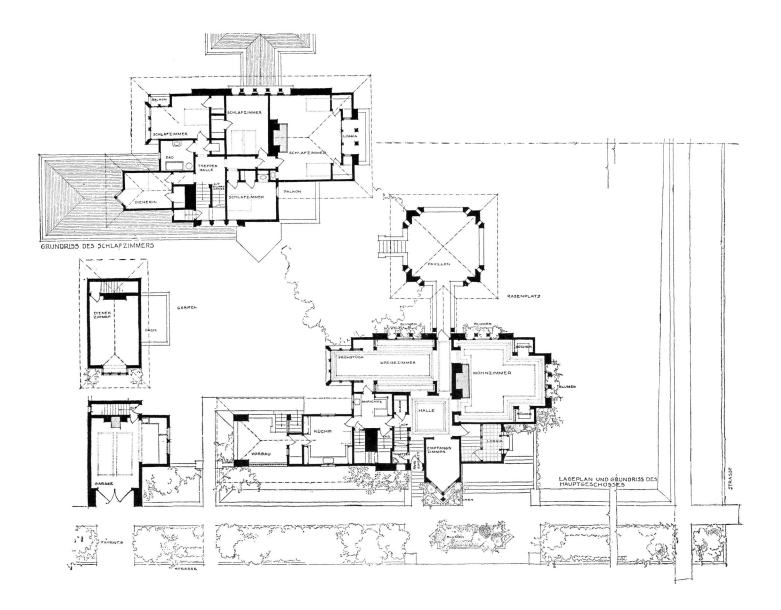

GRUNDRISS DES SCHLAFZIMMERS

LAGEPLAN UND GRUNDRISS DES
HAUPTGESCHOSSES

EMMA MARTIN HOUSE, OAK PARK, ILL. PLANS: MAIN FLOOR AND UPPER FLOOR

EMMA MARTIN HOUSE, OAK PARK, ILL. PAVILION SIDE AND GARDEN SIDE

EMMA MARTIN HOUSE, OAK PARK, ILL. STREET SIDE

P. A. BEACHY HOUSE, OAK PARK, ILL. 1906. GARDEN SIDE

P. A. BEACHY HOUSE, OAK PARK, ILL.
(ABOVE) GARDEN SIDE AND (BELOW) STREET SIDE

W. R. HEATH HOUSE, BUFFALO, N.Y. 1905

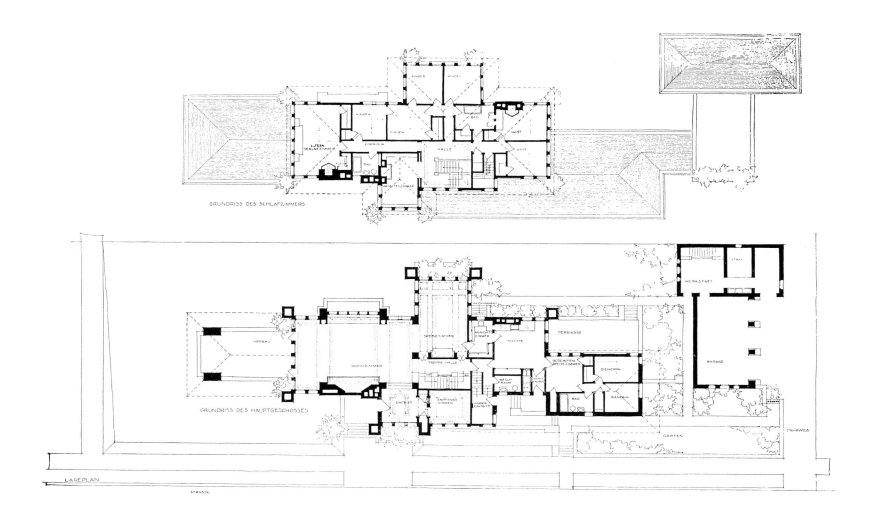

GRUNDRISS DES SCHLAFZIMMERS

GRUNDRISS DES HAUPTGESCHOSSES

LAGEPLAN

W. R. HEATH HOUSE, BUFFALO, N.Y.
PLANS: (ABOVE) UPPER FLOOR AND (BELOW) MAIN FLOOR

W. R. HEATH HOUSE, BUFFALO, N.Y. DETAILS OF ENTRANCE SIDE

W. R. HEATH HOUSE, BUFFALO, N.Y. LIVING ROOM

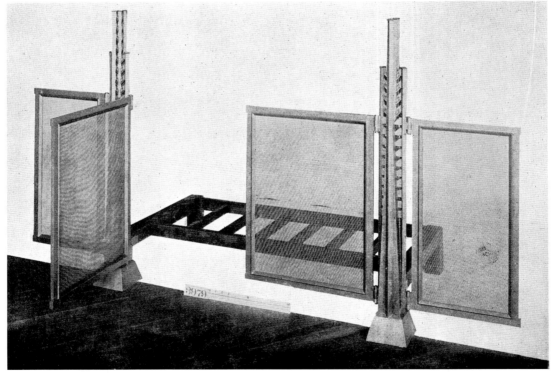

(ABOVE) W. R. HEATH HOUSE, BUFFALO, N.Y. FIREPLACE
(BELOW) SUSAN L. DANA HOUSE, SPRINGFIELD, ILL. FIRE SCREEN

(ABOVE) ROBERT W. EVANS HOUSE, CHICAGO, ILL. FIREPLACE IN LIVING ROOM
(BELOW) B. HARLEY BRADLEY HOUSE, KANKAKEE, ILL. FIREPLACE IN LIVING ROOM

ROBERT W. EVANS HOUSE, CHICAGO, ILL. 1908

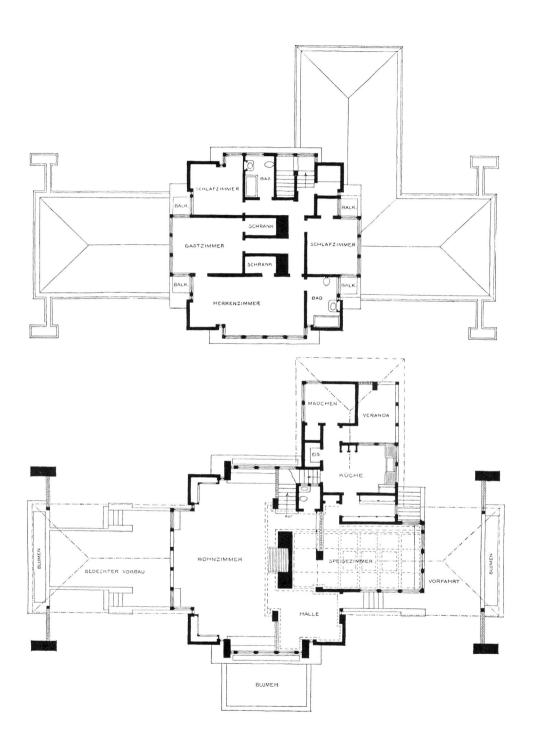

ROBERT W. EVANS HOUSE, CHICAGO, ILL.
PLANS: (ABOVE) MAIN FLOOR AND (BELOW) UPPER FLOOR

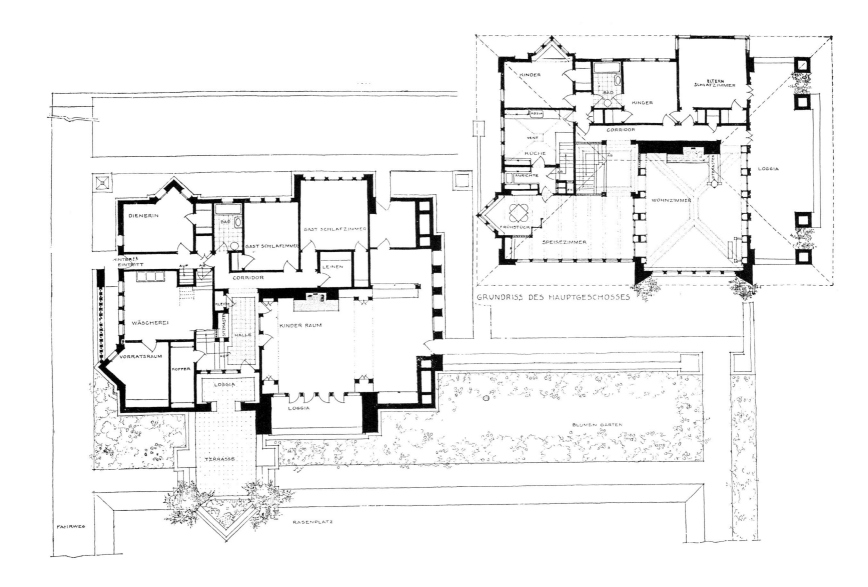

DIENERIN

BAD

GAST SCHLAFZIMMER

GAST SCHLAFZIMMER

HINTERER EINTRITT

AUF

CORRIDOR

LEINEN

KLEIDE

WÄSCHEREI

SITZKASTEN

HALLE

KINDER RAUM

AUF

VORRATSRAUM

KOFFER

LOGGIA

LOGGIA

TERRASSE

FAHRWEG

RASENPLATZ

KINDER

BAD

KINDER

ELTERN SCHLAFZIMMER

CORRIDOR

VENT

KÜCHE

ANRICHTE

WOHNZIMMER

LOGGIA

FRÜHSTÜCK

SPEISEZIMMER

GRUNDRISS DES HAUPTGESCHOSSES

BLUMEN GARTEN

ARTHUR HEURTLEY HOUSE, OAK PARK, ILL. 1902
PLANS: GROUND FLOOR AND UPPER FLOOR

86

ARTHUR HEURTLEY HOUSE, OAK PARK, ILL.
STREET SIDE AND UPPER HALLWAY

ARTHUR HEURTLEY HOUSE, OAK PARK, ILL. NORTH SIDE AND SOUTH SIDE

ARTHUR HEURTLEY HOUSE, OAK PARK, ILL. STREET SIDE

MEYER MAY HOUSE, GRAND RAPIDS, MICH. 1908
DINING ROOM AND FIREPLACE IN LIVING ROOM

MEYER MAY HOUSE, GRAND RAPIDS, MICH.

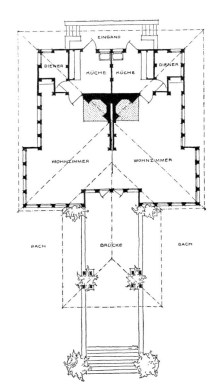

GEORGE E. GERTS HOUSE, DOUBLE RESIDENCE, WHITEHALL, MICH. 1902. VIEW AND PLAN

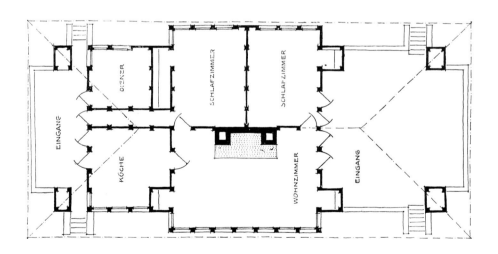

WALTER GERTS HOUSE, WHITEHALL, MICH. 1902. VIEW AND PLAN

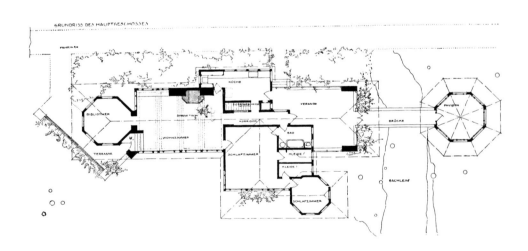

W. A. GLASNER HOUSE, GLENCOE, ILL. 1905. VIEW AND PLAN

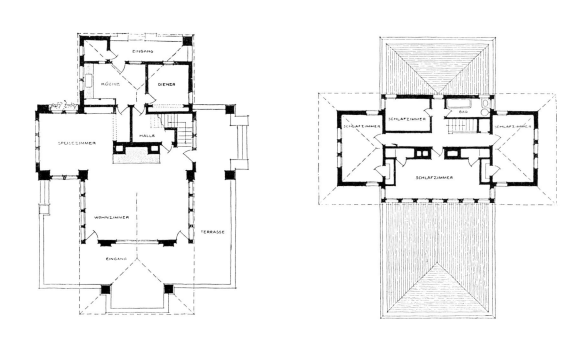

CHARLES S. ROSS HOUSE, LAKE DELAVAN, WIS. 1902. VIEW AND PLANS

FRANK J. BAKER HOUSE, WILMETTE, ILL. 1909. STREET SIDE

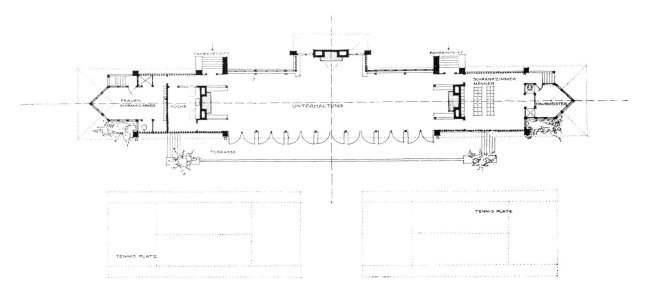

RIVER FOREST TENNIS CLUB, RIVER FOREST, ILL. 1906. VIEW AND PLAN

FRANK LLOYD WRIGHT STUDIO, OAK PARK, ILL. 1889
PORTRAIT FIGURE, RICHARD BOCK, SCULPTOR

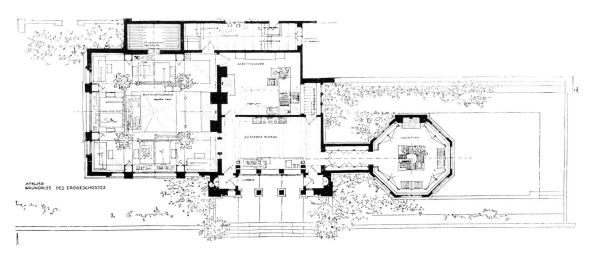

FRANK LLOYD WRIGHT STUDIO, OAK PARK, ILL.
OUTSIDE OFFICE AND PLAN

BROWNE'S BOOKSTORE, CHICAGO, ILL. 1908

EXHIBITION OF DRAWINGS AND MODELS AT ART INSTITUTE, CHICAGO, ILL. 1907

EXHIBITION OF DRAWINGS AND MODELS AT ART INSTITUTE, CHICAGO, ILL.

102

EXHIBITION OF DRAWINGS AND MODELS AT ART INSTITUTE, CHICAGO, ILL.

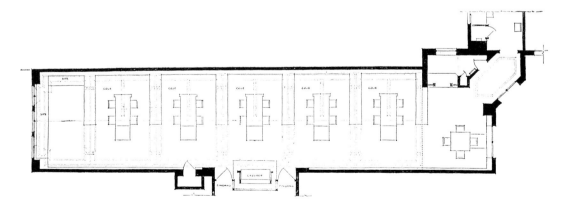

BROWNE'S BOOKSTORE, CHICAGO, ILL. PLAN

(ABOVE) BROWNE'S BOOKSTORE, CHICAGO, ILL. DETAIL
(BELOW) FRANK LLOYD WRIGHT STUDIO, OAK PARK, ILL. ENTRANCE DETAIL

104

(ABOVE) BROWNE'S BOOKSTORE, CHICAGO, ILL. CASHIER'S DESK
(BELOW) FRANK LLOYD WRIGHT STUDIO, OAK PARK, ILL. ENTRANCE

(ABOVE) BROWNE'S BOOKSTORE, CHICAGO, ILL. DETAIL
(BELOW) FRANK LLOYD WRIGHT STUDIO, OAK PARK, ILL. LIBRARY

BROWNE'S BOOKSTORE, CHICAGO, ILL.
(ABOVE) ENTRANCE AND (BELOW) READING ROOM

FRANK LLOYD WRIGHT STUDIO, OAK PARK, ILL.

W. SCOTT THURBER ART GALLERY, CHICAGO, ILL. 1909

UNIVERSAL PORTLAND CEMENT CO. EXHIBIT, MADISON SQUARE GARDEN, N.Y. 1910
CEMENT AND TILES

FREDERICK C. ROBIE HOUSE, CHICAGO, ILL. 1908. SOUTH SIDE

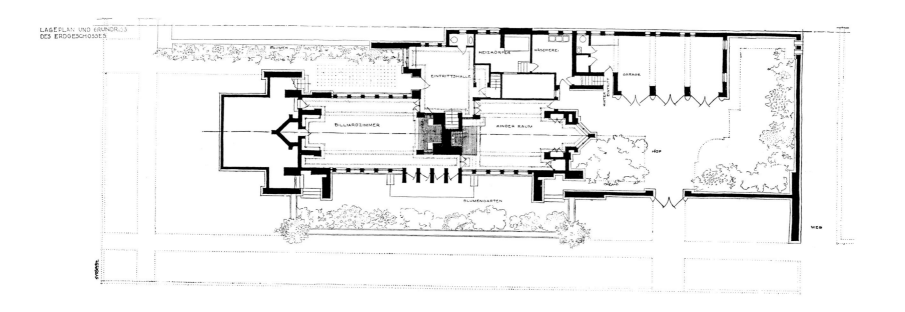

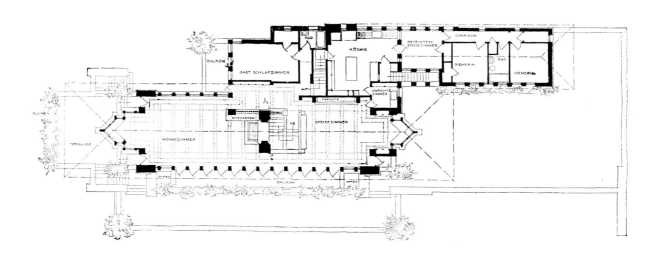

FREDERICK C. ROBIE HOUSE, CHICAGO, ILL.
PLANS: (ABOVE) GROUND FLOOR AND (BELOW) MAIN FLOOR

(ABOVE) FREDERICK C. ROBIE HOUSE, CHICAGO, ILL. LIVING ROOM
(BELOW) AVERY COONLEY HOUSE, RIVERSIDE, ILL. FIREPLACE

FREDERICK C. ROBIE HOUSE, CHICAGO, ILL. DINING ROOM

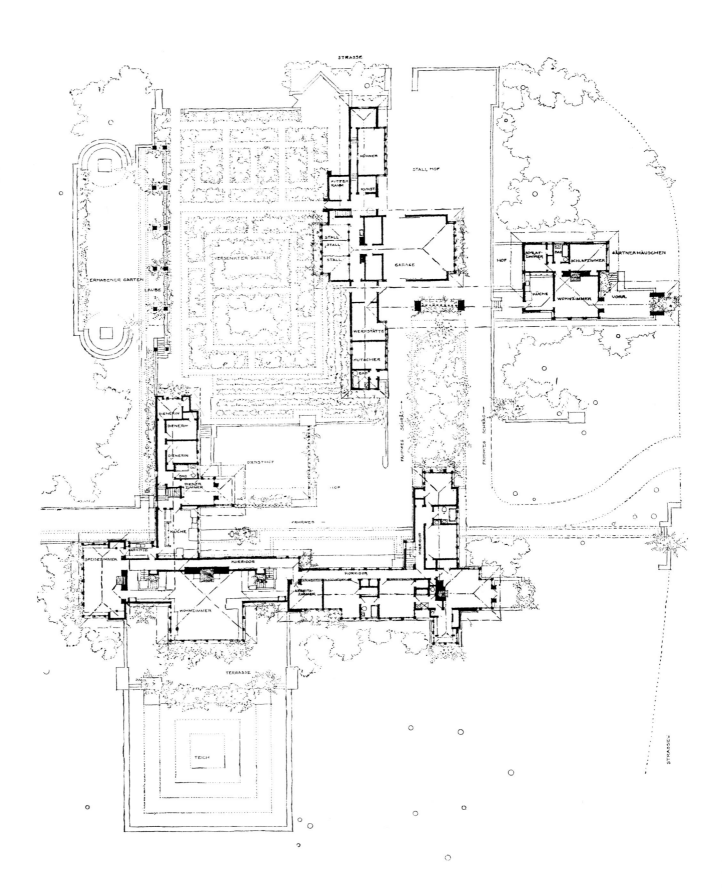

AVERY COONLEY HOUSE, RIVERSIDE, ILL. 1908. SITE PLAN

AVERY COONLEY HOUSE, RIVERSIDE, ILL. LIVING ROOM WING AND TERRACE

AVERY COONLEY HOUSE, RIVERSIDE, ILL.
DINING ROOM, LIVING ROOM AND BEDROOM WINGS CONNNECTED BY GALLERIES

AVERY COONLEY HOUSE, RIVERSIDE, ILL. DETAILS

AVERY COONLEY HOUSE, RIVERSIDE, ILL. GUEST ROOM WING

AVERY COONLEY HOUSE, RIVERSIDE, ILL.
GALLERIES WITH OVERHEAD LIGHTS, LIVING ROOM IN CENTER
EXTERIOR, DRESSING ROOM

AVERY COONLEY HOUSE, RIVERSIDE, ILL. DETAIL OF TERRACE

122

AVERY COONLEY, RIVERSIDE, ILL.
(ABOVE) INTERIOR COURT AND (BELOW) ENTRANCE COURT (COLORED TILE ON WALLS)

123

AVERY COONLEY HOUSE, RIVERSIDE, ILL.
(ABOVE) LIVING ROOM
(BELOW) EXTERIOR, DRESSING ROOM AND GUEST ROOM WINGS

AVERY COONLEY HOUSE, RIVERSIDE, ILL.
VIEW FROM LIVING ROOM THROUGH GALLERY
TOWARD DINING ROOM

OVERHEAD LIGHTS THROUGH
WOOD PANELING IN LIVING ROOM

AVERY COONLEY HOUSE, RIVERSIDE, ILL. GENERAL VIEW

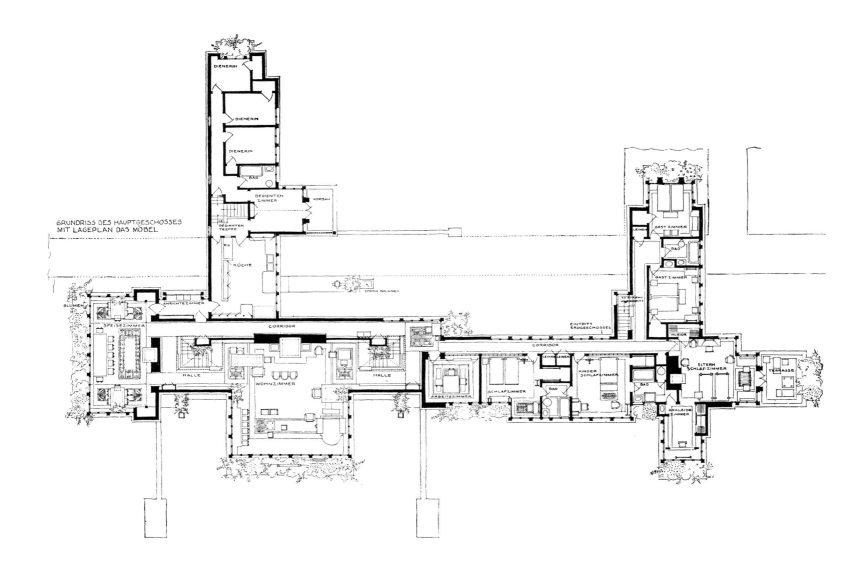

GRUNDRISS DES HAUPTGESCHOSSES
MIT LAGEPLAN DAS MÖBEL

AVERY COONLEY HOUSE, RIVERSIDE, ILL. PLAN OF MAIN FLOOR

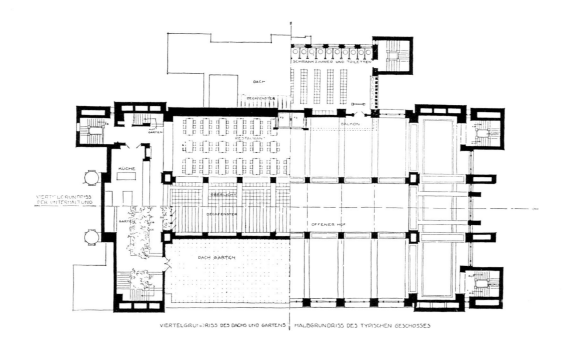

VIERTELGRU.DRISS DES DACHS UND GARTENS | HALBGRUNDRISS DES TYPISCHEN GESCHOSSES

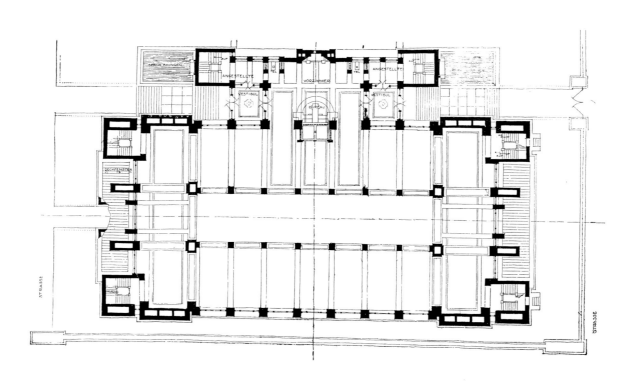

LARKIN CO. ADMINISTRATION BUILDING, BUFFALO, N.Y. 1903. PLANS

LARKIN CO. ADMINISTRATION BUILDING, BUFFALO, N.Y.

LARKIN CO. ADMINISTRATION BUILDING, BUFFALO, N.Y. INTERIOR HALL

LARKIN CO. ADMINISTRATION BUILDING, BUFFALO, N.Y. FRONT VIEW ON SENECA STREET

131

LARKIN CO. ADMINISTRATION BUILDING, BUFFALO, N.Y.
PARTIAL VIEW OF UPPER GALLERY. BRICK, MAGNESITE AND METAL

LARKIN CO. ADMINISTRATION BUILDING, BUFFALO, N.Y.
(ABOVE) VIEW OF DIRECTOR'S AND ADMINISTRATION OFFICES
(BELOW) INFORMATION DESK IN ENTRANCE HALL

LARKIN CO. ADMINISTRATION BUILDING, BUFFALO, N.Y.
VIEW OF AN OFFICE. FURNITURE MADE OF METAL AND MAGNESITE

LARKIN CO. ADMINISTRATION BUILDING, BUFFALO, N.Y.
WATER FOUNTAIN AT ENTRANCE AND DETAILS

LARKIN CO. ADMINISTRATION BUILDING, BUFFALO, N.Y.
VIEWS OF ONE OF THE FLOORS DURING AND AFTER BUSINESS HOURS

LARKIN CO. ADMINISTRATION BUILDING, BUFFALO, N.Y.
EXAMPLES OF OFFICE APPOINTMENTS

METAL FURNITURE, DOUBLE
WINDOWS WITH METAL FRAMES,
METAL FILES BELOW WINDOWS

LARKIN CO. ADMINISTRATION BUILDING, BUFFALO, N.Y.
TYPICAL ARRANGEMENT OF ONE OF THE FLOORS, VIEW TOWARD CENTRAL HALL

LARKIN CO. ADMINISTRATION BUILDING, BUFFALO, N.Y.
(ABOVE) ENTRANCE TO EMPLOYEES' RECREATION ROOM
(BELOW) GALLERY WITH WRITING DESKS FOR VISITORS

LARKIN CO. ADMINISTRATION BUILDING, BUFFALO, N.Y.
FRONT VIEW ON SENECA STREET

LARKIN CO. ADMINISTRATION BUILDING, BUFFALO, N.Y.
CONSTRUCTION DETAIL

GLOSSARY OF TERMS

AB: DOWN
ABHANG: SLOPE
ABSATZ: STAIR LANDING, STEP
ABZUG: EXHAUST
ANFAHRT: ENTRANCE
ANGESTELLTE: EMPLOYEES
ANKLEIDEZIMMER: DRESSING ROOM
ANRICHTE, ANRICHTEZIMMER: PANTRY
ANSICHT: VIEW
ARBEITSTISCH: WORK TABLE
ARBEITSZIMMER: STUDY
AUF: UP
AUFBEWAHRUNGSORT: STORAGE AREA
AUSGANG: EXIT
AUSSENANSICHT: EXTERIOR VIEW
ÄUSSERES BUREAU: OUTER OFFICE
AUSSTELLUNG: EXHIBIT

BACH, BÄCHLEIN: BROOK
BÄCKEREI: BAKERY
BAD: BATH
BADSTRAND: BATHING BEACH
BALKON: BALCONY
BALKON HERÜBER: BALCONY ACROSS
BANK: BENCH, BANK
BANKGEBÄUDE: BANK BUILDING
BAUM: TREE
BEDECKT: COVERED
BEDIENTEN: SERVANTS
BERGQUELL: MOUNTAIN SPRING
BERIESELUNGSGRABEN: IRRIGATION DITCH
BETON: CONCRETE
BIBLIOTHEK: LIBRARY
BILDSÄULE: STATUE
BILLIARDZIMMER: BILLIARD ROOM
BLUMEN: FLOWERS
BLUMENBEET: FLOWER BED
BLUMENGARTEN: FLOWER GARDEN
BOGEN: ARCH
BOGENGANG: ARCHWAY
BOOTE: BOATS
BRENNHOLZ: FIREWOOD
BRÜCKE: BRIDGE
BRUNNEN: WELL, FOUNTAIN
BÜCHER: BOOKS
BÜCHEREI, BÜCHERZIMMER: LIBRARY
BUDE: BOOTH
BUREAU: OFFICE

CASSIERER: CASHIER
CHOR: CHOIR
CLOSET: TOILET
COJE: BOOTH

DACH: ROOF
DACHFENSTER: SKYLIGHT
DACHGARTEN: ROOF GARDEN
DARÜBER: ABOVE
DECKFENSTER: SKYLIGHT
DEICH: DAM
DIENER: MANSERVANT
DIENERIN: MAID
DIENERINZIMMER: MAID'S ROOM
DIENERZIMMER: SERVANT'S ROOM
DIENSTEINTRITT: SERVANT'S ENTRANCE
DIENSTHOF: SERVANT'S COURTYARD
DIENSTTREPPE: SERVANT'S STAIRCASE, BACKSTAIRS

DIREKTION: MANAGEMENT
DRUCKEREI: PRINT SHOP
DUNKELRAUM: DARKROOM

EIGENES ZIMMER: PRIVATE ROOM
EINLAGE: INLAY
EINLEITENDER ENTWURF: PRELIMINARY SKETCH
EINRAUMUNG: BAY
EINSTÖCKIG: ONE-STORY
EINTRITT: ENTRANCE
EINTRITTSHALLE: ENTRANCE HALL
EINZELHEIT: DETAIL
EIS: ICE
ELTERN SCHLAFZIMMER: PARENTS' BEDROOM
EMPFANGSHALLE: RECEPTION HALL
EMPFANGSZIMMER: RECEPTION ROOM
ENTWURFSZIMMER: DRAFTING ROOM
ERDGESCHOSS: GROUND FLOOR
ERHABEN: RAISED, ELEVATED
ERHOLUNGSRAUM: RECREATION ROOM
ERSTER TEIL: FIRST PART
ESSTISCH: DINING TABLE
ESSZIMMER: DINING ROOM

FAHREINTRITT: ENTRANCE DRIVE
FAHRRÄDER: BICYCLES
FAHRSTUHL: ELEVATOR
FAHRWEG: DRIVEWAY
FAHRWEG SCHRÄG: SLOPING DRIVEWAY
FENSTER: WINDOW
FESTSAAL: BANQUET HALL
FEUERFESTES GEWÖLBE: FIREPROOF VAULT
FEUERRAUM: FURNACE ROOM
FLUSS: RIVER
FRAUEN: WOMEN
FRÜHSTÜCK: BREAKFAST
FUNDAMENT: FOUNDATION
FUTTERRAUM: FODDER STORAGE AREA

GALERIE: GALLERY
GALERIE HERÜBER: GALLERY ACROSS
GARDEROBE: CLOAKROOM
GARTEN: GARDEN
GÄRTNERHÄUSCHEN: GARDENER'S COTTAGE
GASSE: ALLEYWAY
GASTZIMMER: GUEST ROOM
GEDÄCHTNISNISCHE: MEMORIAL NICHE
GEGEN SÜDEN: SOUTHWARD
GEHEGE: ENCLOSURE
GEMEINTREPPE: COMMON STAIRCASE
GERÄTE: TOOLS
GESCHOSS: FLOOR, STORY
GEWÄCHSHAUS: GREENHOUSE
GEWÖLBE: VAULT
GITTERWERK: LATTICE WORK
GRUNDRISS: PLAN, FLOOR PLAN

HALB: HALF
HALBKREIS: SEMI-CIRCLE
HALLE: HALL
HAUPTGESCHOSS: MAIN FLOOR
HAUS-WISSENSCHAFT: DOMESTIC SCIENCE DEPARTMENT
HÄUSERBLOCK: BLOCK OF HOUSES
HAUSHÄLTERIN: HOUSEKEEPER
HAUSMEISTER: CARETAKER
HEIZKÖRPER: RADIATOR, HEATING
HEIZUNG: HEATING PLANT

HINTEREINTRITT: REAR ENTRANCE
HINTERHOF: BACKYARD
HOF: COURTYARD
HÖHE DES ERDBODENS: GROUND LEVEL
HÖHERER TEIL: UPPER PART
HÖRSAAL: AUDITORIUM
HÜHNER: CHICKENS
HÜHNERHAUS: CHICKEN COOP
HÜHNERHOF: CHICKEN YARD

IM FREIEN: OUTDOORS
INNERES: INTERIOR

KAMIN: FIREPLACE
KASSENGEHILFE: BANK CLERK, TELLER
KELLER: CELLAR, BASEMENT
KINDER: CHILDREN
KINDERFRAU-ZIMMER: GOVERNESS'S ROOM
KINDERRAUM, KINDERSTUBE, KINDERZIMMER: CHILDREN'S ROOM
KINDER SCHLAFZIMMER: CHILDREN'S BEDROOM
KLASSE: CLASSROOM
KLAVIER: PIANO
KLEIDER: CLOTHES
KLOSTER: CLOISTER
KLUBHAUS: CLUBHOUSE
KOFFER: LUGGAGE
KOHLE: COAL
KOMMIS: CLERKS
KONZERTZIMMER: MUSIC ROOM
KÜCHE: KITCHEN
KÜCHENGARTEN: KITCHEN GARDEN
KÜHLRAUM: COLD STORAGE ROOM
KUHSTALL: COW BARN
KUNSTGEWERBE: HANDICRAFT
KÜNSTLERHAUS: ARTIST'S HOUSE
KUNSTSCHULE: ART SCHOOL
KUTSCHER: COACHMAN

LADEN: STORE
LADENTISCH: COUNTER
LAGEPLAN: SITE PLAN
LANDHAUS: COUNTRY HOUSE
LAUBE: ARBOR
LEINEN: LINEN
LESEZIMMER: READING ROOM
LICHT: LIGHT
LICHTSCHACHT: LIGHT WELL
LÖSUNG: SOLUTION

MÄNNER: MEN
MAUER: WALL
MEER: SEA
MIETSHAUS: APARTMENT HOUSE
MÖBEL: FURNITURE

NÄHSTUBE: SEWING ROOM

OBER: UPPER
OBERGESCHOSS: UPPER FLOOR
OBERLICHT: SKYLIGHT
OFEN: STOVE, OVEN
OFFEN: OPEN
ORGEL: ORGAN

PFARRER: PASTOR
PFLEGERIN-ZIMMER: NURSE'S ROOM
PRIVAT BUREAU: PRIVATE OFFICE

QUERSCHNITT: SECTION

RASENPLATZ: LAWN AREA
RAUM: ROOM, AREA
RAUM F. D. GEDÄCHTNISFEIER: ROOM FOR MEMORIAL SERVICE
RECHTECKIG: RECTANGULAR
REDNERBÜHNE: SPEAKER'S PLATFORM
RETTUNGSLEITER: ESCAPE LADDER

SAAL: HALL
SCHEMA: SCHEME
SCHLAF VERANDA: SLEEPING PORCH
SCHLAFZIMMER: BEDROOM
SCHLUCHT: RAVINE
SCHRANK: CLOSET, WARDROBE
SCHRANKZIMMER: LOCKER ROOM, CLOSET ROOM
SCHÜLERSCHRÄNKE: PUPILS' LOCKERS
SCHUPPEN: BARN
SCHWIMMENDE LANDUNGSBRÜCKE: FLOATING DOCK
SEE: LAKE
SEITENBAU: WING
SICHERHEITSGEWÖLBE: SAFETY VAULT
SITZKASTEN: BENCH, SEAT
SOMMER-WOHNSITZ: SUMMER HOME
SONNTAGSSCHULE: SUNDAY SCHOOL
SPEISESAAL: DINING HALL
SPEISEZIMMER: DINING ROOM
SPIELPLATZ: PLAYGROUND
SPRINGBRUNNEN: FOUNTAIN
STÄDTISCHES WOHNHAUS: TOWN HOUSE
STALL: STABLE
STALLGEBÄUDE: STABLE BUILDING
STALLHOF: STABLE YARD
STEINSCHAFT: STONE SHAFT
STEINSCHNITT: CARVED STONE, CUT STONE
STRASSE: STREET
STUFE: STEP

TANZSAAL: DANCE HALL
TEICH: POND
TELEFONZELLE: TELEPHONE BOOTH
TERRASSE: TERRACE
TIEF: DEEP
TISCH: TABLE
TOILETTEN: TOILETS
TREPPE: STAIRCASE
TREPPENHALLE: STAIR HALL
TURM: TOWER
TURNHALLE: GYMNASIUM
TYPISCH: TYPICAL

ÜBER: ABOVE
UNTER: UNDER, LOWER
UNTERIRDISCHER GANG: UNDERGROUND PASSAGE
UNTIEF: SHALLOW
URNE: URN

VEREINSZIMMER: CLUB ROOM
VERSAMMLUNGSSAAL: ASSEMBLY HALL
VERSENKT: SUNKEN
VIERTEL: QUARTER
VORBAU: PORCH
VORDERFRONT: FACADE
VORORT: SUBURB
VORRATSRAUM: PANTRY, LARDER
VORSTADTHAUS: SUBURBAN HOUSE
VORZIMMER: ANTE-ROOM

WAGENREMISE: CARRIAGE HOUSE
WÄSCHEREI: LAUNDRY
WASCHRAUM: LAVATORY
WEG: ROAD, PATH
WERKSTATT: WORKSHOP
WOHNHAUS: DWELLING
WOHNUNG: APARTMENT
WOHNUNGSSAAL: DRAWING ROOM
WOHNUNGSZIMMER, WOHNZIMMER: LIVING ROOM

ZIMMER: ROOM
ZU DEN, ZUM, ZUR: TO THE
ZWEI: TWO
ZWEITER TEIL: SECOND PART
ZWISCHENSTOCK: MEZZANINE